KYRGYZ REPUBLIC 2016 HUMAN RIGHTS REPORT

EXECUTIVE SUMMARY

The Kyrgyz Republic has a parliamentary form of government designed to limit presidential power and enhance the role of parliament and the prime minister. On December 11, a national referendum on constitutional reform was held in conjunction with municipal elections. An overwhelming majority (79.6 percent) voted in favor of the amendments with 38.84 percent voter turnout. In October 2015 voters elected new members of parliament in peaceful elections. Observers, including the Organization for Security and Cooperation in Europe (OSCE), concluded the election was competitive, advancing the country's democratic development, although it was not without procedural shortcomings. In 2011 then Prime Minister Almazbek Atambaev won the presidential election with 63 percent of the vote. Independent observers considered that election transparent and competitive, despite some irregularities.

Civilian authorities at times did not maintain effective control over the security forces, particularly in the provinces of Jalal-Abad and Osh.

The most significant human rights problems reported included violations of fundamental procedural protections throughout the judicial process; the harassment of local nongovernmental organizations (NGOs), activists, and journalists; and attacks, threats, and systematic police-driven extortion of sexual and ethnic minority groups.

Other problems included substandard prison conditions; allegations of law enforcement officers' use of arbitrary arrest and torture; pressure on independent media; restrictions on religious freedom; pervasive corruption; discrimination and violence against women, persons with disabilities, ethnic and religious minorities, and persons based on their sexual orientation or gender identity; child abuse; trafficking in persons, including forced labor; and child labor.

While authorities investigated reports of official abuse in the security services and elsewhere, they rarely or successfully prosecuted and punished officials accused of human rights violations, or complicity in trafficking. Impunity was a major problem.

Section 1. Respect for the Integrity of the Person, Including Freedom from:

a. Arbitrary Deprivation of Life and other Unlawful or Politically Motivated Killings

There were no reports the government or its agents purposely committed arbitrary or unlawful killings in 2016.

On February 16, Ombudsman of the Kyrgyz Republic Kubat Otorbayev announced that his office had taken over the investigation into the deaths of three inmates while in police custody. In October 2015 nine prison inmates convicted of "Islamic extremism" escaped prison and killed three state penitentiary officers while fleeing. Authorities quickly recaptured five of the inmates, three of whom died shortly after their return to prison due to "heart conditions and other medical issues." Authorities shot and killed the remaining four escapees during police operations to recapture them. Some human rights activists claimed the prisoners' deaths in custody resulted from torture. Family members asserted the prisoners had been in good health.

b. Disappearance

There were no reports of politically motivated disappearances, but local and international observers indicated there continued to be cases in the southern part of the country of holding detainees incommunicado for lengthy periods.

c. Torture and Other Cruel, Inhuman, or Degrading Treatment or Punishment

The law prohibits torture and other cruel, inhuman, or degrading treatment or punishment. Unlike in the previous year, there were no prominent reports of alleged torture by security force personnel; nonetheless, police abuse remained a problem. Physical abuse, including inhuman and degrading treatment, reportedly continued in prisons. The ombudsman said that for the first half of the year, his office received 37 alleged torture complaint cases.

As in 2015 defense attorneys, journalists, and human rights monitoring organizations, including Golos Svobody, Bir Duino, and the international NGO Human Rights Watch (HRW), reported incidents of serious abuse or torture by police and other law enforcement agencies. NGOs stated that the government established strong torture-monitoring bodies, but the independence of these bodies was under threat.

Golos Svobody played a central role monitoring allegations of torture and was the central organizer of the Anti-Torture Coalition, a consortium of 18 NGOs that continued to work with the Prosecutor General's Office to track complaints of torture. The Prosecutor General's Office indicated it received 231 torture complaints in the first half of the year.

The Anti-Torture Coalition also accepted complaints of torture and passed them to the Prosecutor General's Office to facilitate investigations. The coalition reported that, for the first eight months of the year, it received 86 complaints of torture. According to members of the Anti-torture Coalition, the cases it submitted against alleged torturers did not lead to convictions. In historical cases where police were put on trial for torture, prosecutors, judges, and defendants routinely raised procedural and substantive objections, delaying the cases, often resulting in stale evidence, and ultimately leading to case dismissal. NGOs reported that courts regularly included into evidence confessions allegedly induced through torture.

Defense lawyers stated that, once prosecutors took a case to trial, a conviction was almost certain. According to Golos Svobody, investigators often took two weeks or longer to review torture claims, at which point the physical evidence of torture was no longer visible. Defense attorneys presented most allegations of torture during trial proceedings, and the courts typically rejected them. In some cases detainees who filed torture complaints later recanted, reportedly in the face of intimidation by law enforcement officers.

As of year's end, the Osh regional court had not scheduled a hearing on the appeal of the dismissal of torture charges against police. In January 2015 police were accused of torturing three suspects in the theft of 339 million som ($4.9 million) from the Osh airport because the suspects allegedly refused to pay a bribe to secure their own release.

Prison and Detention Center Conditions

Prison conditions were harsh and sometimes life threatening due to food and medicine shortages, substandard health care, lack of heat, and mistreatment.

There were no significant reports regarding private detention facilities for migrants and asylum seekers or detention center conditions for disabled persons that raised human rights concerns.

<u>Physical Conditions</u>: Pretrial and temporary detention facilities were particularly overcrowded, and conditions and mistreatment generally were worse than in prisons. Authorities generally held juveniles separately from adults but grouped them in overcrowded temporary detention centers when other facilities were unavailable. Convicted prisoners occasionally remained in pretrial detention centers while their cases were under appeal.

An NGO representative reported that in some cases prison gangs controlled prison management and discipline, since prison officials lacked the capacity and expertise in running a facility. In some instances the gangs controlled items that could be brought into the prison, such as food and clothing, while prison officials looked the other way. According to NGOs, authorities did not try to dismantle these groups because they were too powerful and believed that removing them could lead to chaos. Some prisoners indicated that prison order and safety was left to the prison gangs or prisoners themselves, resulting in instances of violence and intimidation among inmates.

<u>Administration</u>: Persons held in pretrial detention often did not have access to visitors. Prisoners have the right to file complaints with prison officials or with higher authorities. According to the NGO Bir Duino, prison staff inconsistently reported and documented complaints. Many observers believed that the official number of prisoner complaints of mistreatment represented only a small fraction of the actual cases.

<u>Independent Monitoring</u>: NGO leaders reported prison officials increased openness to allowing monitors into prison and detention facilities, and most monitoring groups reported receiving unfettered access, including the International Committee of the Red Cross (ICRC). Some NGOs, including Bir Duino and Spravedlivost, had the right to visit prisons independently as part of their provision of technical assistance, such as medical and psychological care.

The Red Cross faced no restrictions on whom they could visit. Their visits were unannounced, and they could meet privately with detainees, who reportedly were candid about their conditions. While the ICRC operated under a memorandum of understanding with authorities, and there is no domestic legislation explicitly permitting their activities, they reported good government support.

The National Center to Prevent Torture and other Inhuman and Offensive Treatment and Punishment, an independent and impartial body, is empowered to monitor detention facilities. The center consists of 11 government employees spread across seven offices and empowered to make unannounced, unfettered visits to detention facilities. NGO representatives stated that center officials made progress monitoring and documenting some violations in detention facilities, but they stressed that a standardized approach to identifying torture cases, along with additional resources and staff members, were necessary to conduct its work.

The Prosecutor General's Office created an independent office in July 2015 to investigate and prosecute torture. The independent office is centrally located, facilitating the use of prosecutors not involved directly with the region where the alleged torture may have taken place. Observers believed the investigators would be less subject to local pressures that might prevent proper investigation of a case

d. Arbitrary Arrest or Detention

While the law prohibits arbitrary arrest, in practice it occurred. Human rights organizations in Osh reported arrests unfairly targeting ethnic Uzbeks for alleged involvement in banned religious organizations and for alleged "religious extremism activity." Arrests for lack of proper identification documents were common. Attorneys reported that police frequently arrested individuals on false charges and then solicited bribes in exchange for release.

Role of the Police and Security Apparatus

The investigation of general and local crimes falls under the authority of the Ministry of Internal Affairs, while national-level crimes fall under the authority of the State Committee for National Security (GKNB). The GKNB also controls the presidential security service. The Prosecutor General's Office prosecutes both local and national crimes.

Both local and international observers said law enforcement officers engaged in widespread arbitrary arrests, detainee abuse, and extortion, particularly in the southern part of the country. Authorities dismissed or prosecuted few Ministry of Internal Affairs officials for corruption or abuse of authority.

NGOs and other legal observers routinely noted the lack of ethnic minorities in the police force and in all government positions. Officially, ethnic minorities (non-ethnic Kyrgyz) made up approximately 4.7 percent of the police force. According to UN statistics, ethnic minorities constituted approximately 27 percent of the population.

Arrest Procedures and Treatment of Detainees

According to the criminal procedure code, only courts have the authority to issue search and seizure warrants. While prosecutors have the burden of proof in persuading a judge that a defendant should be detained pending trial, activists reported detention without a warrant remained common. NGOs reported that police targeted vulnerable defendants from whom they believed they could secure a bribe. Observers alleged incidents in which police targeted ethnic Uzbeks by planting literature and then charging them with possession of banned religious materials. Authorities could legally hold a detainee for 48 to 72 hours before filing charges; authorities generally respected these limits. The law requires investigators to notify a detainee's family of the detention within 12 hours, but officials inconsistently enforced this provision. Following official charges, the courts have discretion to hold a suspect in pretrial detention for as much as one year, after which they are legally required to release the suspect. There is a functioning bail system, but there are no other alternatives to the bail system under the law.

Persons arrested or charged with a crime have the right to defense counsel at public expense. By law the accused has the right to consult with defense counsel immediately upon arrest or detention, but in many cases the first meeting did not occur until the trial. As in past years, human rights groups noted incidents in which authorities denied attorneys to arrested minors, often holding them without parental notification and questioning them without parents or attorneys present, despite laws forbidding these practices.

The law authorizes the use of house arrest for certain categories of suspects. Reports indicated that law enforcement officers selectively enforced the law by incarcerating persons suspected of minor crimes while not pursuing those suspected of more serious ones.

<u>Arbitrary Arrest</u>: As in previous years, NGOs and monitoring organizations, including Golos Svobody, Bir Duino, HRW, Spravedlivost, the UN Office of the High Commissioner for Human Rights, and the OSCE, recorded complaints of arbitrary arrest. Most observers asserted it was impossible to know the number of cases because the majority went unreported. According to NGOs in the southern part of the country, arrests and harassment of individuals allegedly involved in extremist religious groups--predominantly ethnic Uzbeks--continued.

There were reports of arrests of individuals involved in the banned extremist group Hizb ut-Tahrir, a trend that began to increase in 2014. According to Bir Duino, however, some arrests were driven by corruption within the law enforcement system. Police appeared at homes falsely claiming to have a search warrant. There were allegations police would enter a home, plant printed material promoting Hizb ut-Tahrir, and arrest the suspect in the hope of extracting a bribe to secure release. There was no information on the Supreme Court appeal of the February 2015 arrest of Rashod Kamalov, convicted in October 2015 by the Karasuu District Court of extremist Islamic activity.

Pretrial Detention: According to the penal code, authorities may hold a suspect at a pretrial detention facility during the official investigation. The general legal restriction on the length of investigations is 60 days. Complex legal procedures, poor access to lawyers, and limited investigation capacity often lengthened defendants' time in pretrial detention beyond the 60-day limit, with some being detained legally for as long as one year.

Detainee's Ability to Challenge Lawfulness of Detention before a Court: According to the Kyrgyz Criminal Procedure Code (CPC), individuals may challenge the lawfulness of their detention at any point. The CPC also outlines instances in which restitution may be made to affected individuals or their heirs following a court's determination of unlawful detention. These instances happened extremely rarely.

e. Denial of Fair Public Trial

The law provides for an independent judiciary, but judges were subject to influence or corruption, and there were instances where the outcomes of trials appeared predetermined. Multiple sources, including NGOs, attorneys, government officials, and private citizens, asserted judges paid bribes to attain their positions. Many attorneys asserted that bribe taking was ubiquitous among judges. Authorities generally respected court orders.

Numerous NGOs described pervasive violations of the right to a fair trial, including coerced confessions, use of torture, denial of access to counsel, and convictions in the absence of sufficiently conclusive evidence or despite exculpatory evidence. International observers reported threats and acts of violence against defendants and defense attorneys within and outside the courtroom, as well as intimidation of trial judges by victims' relatives and friends.

On August 8, the president signed the Court Bailiffs Bill into law to enhance the security of the courts.

Azimjon Askarov, an ethnic Uzbek human rights activist convicted of murder along with seven codefendants in the 2010 killing of a Bazar Korgon police officer, remained imprisoned at year's end. In 2012 his attorneys filed a formal complaint or "communication" with the UN Human Rights Committee claiming that the government had denied Askarov a fair trial by withholding evidence, intimidating witnesses, and committing acts of torture. On April 21, the committee issued findings that Askarov had been arbitrarily detained, held in inhuman conditions, tortured and mistreated, and prevented from adequately preparing his defense. The committee called on the government to annul Askarov's conviction, release him immediately, and, if necessary, conduct a new trial. Pursuant to the committee's findings, the Supreme Court convened on July 11 to reconsider Askarov's case.

The government invited diplomats, journalists, representatives of international organizations, and human rights groups to attend the hearing. On July 12, the Supreme Court overturned Askarov's life sentence and remanded the case to the Chui district lower court for additional review. On October 4, the Chui District Court commenced a retrial of the Askarov case, calling several witnesses to testify. Askarov actively participated in the courtroom during these proceedings.

In 2013 the prison service stated it would only allow six visits per year to Askarov. NGO leaders from Bir Duino reported making regular visits to Askarov, however, under an exception that permits local NGOs involved in providing medical, psychological, and other support to visit. Those who visited Askarov reported his physical condition continued to be poor. Because Askarov rejected a physical examination by a government doctor, authorities refused to let other physicians examine him.

Trial Procedures

While the law provides for defendants' rights, the customs and practices of the judicial system regularly contradicted the constitutional presumption of innocence, and pretrial investigations focused on the collection of sufficient evidence to prove guilt. The law requires courts to inform defendants promptly and in detail of the charges against them, and to provide interpreters as needed. Trials were conducted in the state language, Kyrgyz, or the official language, Russian. In a majority of trials, courtroom procedure required defendants to sit in caged cells. There is no protection against double jeopardy.

Defense attorneys complained that judges routinely returned cases to investigators if there was not enough evidence to prove guilt, during which time suspects could remain in detention. Judges, according to attorneys, gave defendants a suspended sentence regardless of how little evidence existed to sustain a prison term.

Trials were generally open to the public, unless they involved state secrets or privacy concerns of defendants, and courts announced verdicts publicly, even in closed proceedings. State prosecutors submit criminal cases to courts, while judges direct criminal proceedings. Criminal cases feature a single judge, while three-judge panels conduct appellate cases. Judges have full authority to render verdicts and determine sentences.

The law provides for unlimited visits between an attorney and a client during trial, but authorities did not always grant permission for such visits. The government provided indigent defendants with attorneys at public expense, and defendants could refuse legal counsel and defend themselves. HRW, domestic NGOs, and local attorneys reported some state-provided criminal defense lawyers were complicit with prosecutors and did not properly defend their clients. Many observers, particularly in the southern part of the country, described these lawyers as "pocket attorneys" who would help secure bribes from their client to pass to police and judges, which would then secure the client's eventual release. International observers reported the quality of representation was much worse in rural areas than in the capital. In many cases, it was difficult for individuals accused of extremism-related crimes to find an attorney who was not closely connected to police.

The law permits defendants and their counsel to attend all proceedings, question witnesses, present evidence, call witnesses, and access prosecution evidence in advance of trial, but courts frequently did not follow these requirements. Witnesses typically were required to testify in person. Under certain circumstances courts allowed testimony via audio or video recording. Defendants and counsel, by law, have the right to communicate freely, in private, with no limitation on the frequency. Defendants and prosecutors have the right to appeal a court's decision. An appellate court can increase a lower court's sentence against a defendant.

Political Prisoners and Detainees

Courts convicted opposition party members and ethnic Uzbeks of politically motivated actions related to violence. In view of outstanding questions surrounding their connection to the violence and the fairness of the trials and appeals, some observers considered them political prisoners.

Civil Judicial Procedures and Remedies

The constitution and law provide for an independent and impartial judiciary in civil matters. As with criminal matters, citizens believed the civil judicial system was subject to influence from the outside, including by the government. Local courts address civil, criminal, economic, administrative, and other cases. The Supreme Court is the highest judicial authority. Article 41 of the constitution guarantees citizens the right to apply in accordance with international treaties to international human rights bodies seeking protection of violated rights and freedoms. In the event these bodies confirm the violation of human rights and freedoms, the government is obligated by the constitution to take measures for their restoration and/or compensation for damage.

f. Arbitrary or Unlawful Interference with Privacy, Family, Home, or Correspondence

The law requires approval from the prosecutor general for wiretaps, home searches, mail interception, and similar acts, including in cases relating to national security. The law states officials should use wiretapping of electronic communications exclusively to combat crime and only with a court order. Eleven government agencies have legal authority to monitor citizens' telephone and internet communications.

According to an NGO, on May 25, approximately 20 court officers visited the home of Khadicha Askarova, wife of imprisoned human rights activist Azimjon Askarov, in Bazar-Korgon, Jalal-Abad province. A court bailiff informed one of Askarova's lawyers that the court had assigned them to make an inventory of the property and house in preparation for its confiscation. According to Askarova, the court officers examined the property without providing documentation of the court order.

The Law on Defense and Armed Forces authorizes the military to confiscate private property for the purpose of state security.

Section 2. Respect for Civil Liberties, Including:

a. Freedom of Speech and Press

The law provides for freedom of speech and press, and citizens generally were free to exercise these rights. Self-censorship, however, was prevalent, and some journalists reported pressure from editors and political figures to bias their reporting on sensitive topics.

Freedom of Speech and Expression: As in earlier years, some journalists reported intimidation related to coverage of sensitive topics, such as interethnic relations, "religious extremism," or the rise of nationalism. The trend was particularly salient against Uzbek-language media outlets. Others felt threatened for reporting critically on public figures. Some journalists admitted to self-censoring their reporting due to fear of reprisals.

Press and Media Freedoms: In recent years, there were attempts to prevent independent media from operating freely in the country. Tight government controls over news content on state television was widely acknowledged. In July the Alamudun District Court blocked the website of journalist Dayirbek Orunbekov and began criminal proceedings against him for not having complied with a previous court order. In December, opposition television station "September" was denied accreditation to cover the President's annual year-end news conference. In a letter delivered to the outlet, the President's Political Information Office explained the decision stemmed from the station's "objectivity in presenting information" and their "involvement in the development of free speech."

There was a small degree of foreign ownership of media through local partners. Russian-language television stations dominated coverage and local ratings. A number of Russia-based media outlets operated freely in the country, and the government treated them as domestic media.

Violence and Harassment: Some journalists were subject to harassment. Following the July blockage of Dayirbek Orunbekov's website, on August 11, an informal group of activists, the Committee to Protect Freedom of Speech, expressed concern with the "political persecution" of Orunbekov, stating that the "life, safety, and freedom of the journalist is under threat, as he receives threatening telephone calls and text messages from unknown people."

<u>Censorship or Content Restrictions</u>: As in previous years, journalists and NGO leaders alleged some news outlets instructed their reporters not to report critically on certain politicians or government officials. The sources also reported some news outlets received requests from offices of the government to report in a particular way or to ignore specific news stories.

NGO leaders and media contacts reported that state-owned broadcasters came under increasing pressure to run stories promoting government policies and initiatives and develop narratives that are critical of NGOs, opposition figures, and civil society activists. In a number of instances, multiple state-owned outlets ran at the same time nearly identical attack pieces on NGO leaders.

<u>Libel/Slander Laws</u>: While libel is not a criminal offense, NGO leaders described the False Accusations Amendments, passed in 2014, as a practical "recriminalizing of libel." Journalists noted the law exposed journalists and the media to libel suits in civil courts that could bankrupt the outlets or journalists. In January 2015, however, the Supreme Court narrowed the reach of the law, holding that henceforth it would only apply in cases of knowingly making false statements in a police report but not to statements in the media.

Freedom House noted "insult" and "insult of public officials" were criminal offenses and that the law is detrimental to the development of freedom of speech and mass media in the country. The head of the Media Policy Institute reported her organization routinely defended journalists charged with libel and slander, and members of the media regularly feared the threat of lawsuits.

Internet Freedom

The government generally allowed access to the internet, including social media sites, and there were no credible reports the government monitored private online communications without appropriate legal authority. Members of the lesbian, gay, bisexual, transgender, and intersex (LGBTI) community reported police regularly monitored LGBTI chat rooms and dating sites and arranged meetings with LGBTI users of the sites in order to extort money from them.

According to the International Telecommunication Union, the internet penetration rate was 30 percent.

According to the Civic Initiative on Internet Policy, with reference to the State Communications Agency, approximately 30 websites remained blocked at year's end. These sites involved groups that the government deemed to be terrorist or extremist, as well as sites advertising sexual services. Four of the sites involved the banned group Hizb ut-Tahrir.

On May 25, parliament passed an amendment to the law on countering extremist activity that authorizes the Ministry of Transport and Communications to block without a court order internet websites spreading extremist and terrorist materials. At year's end there were no reports the government had used this law.

Academic Freedom and Cultural Events

There were no government restrictions on academic freedom. Institutions providing advanced religious education must follow strict reporting policies, but they reported no restrictions on academic freedom.

b. Freedom of Peaceful Assembly and Association

The law provides for freedom of assembly and association, and the government generally respected these rights.

Freedom of Assembly

The constitution provides for this right, and the government generally respected it, with some exceptions. Organizers and participants are responsible for notifying authorities of planned assemblies, but the constitution prohibits authorities from banning or restricting peaceful assemblies, even in the absence of prior notification. Local authorities, however, have the right to demand an end to a public action and, in the event of noncompliance, are empowered to take measures to end assemblies.

Freedom of Association

The law provides for freedom of association, and the government generally respected it. NGOs, labor unions, political parties, and cultural associations must register with the Ministry of Justice. NGOs are required to have at least three members, and all other organizations at least 10 members. The Ministry of Justice did not refuse to register any domestic NGOs. The law prohibits foreign-funded political parties and NGOs, including their representative offices and branches, from pursuing political goals.

The government continued to maintain bans on approximately 20 "religiously oriented" groups it considered to be extremist, including al-Qaida, the Taliban, the Islamic Movement of Eastern Turkistan, the Kurdish People's Congress, the Organization for the Liberation of Eastern Turkistan, Hizb ut-Tahrir (HT), the Union of Islamic Jihad, the Islamic Party of Turkistan, the Unification (Mun San Men) Church, Takfir Jihadist, Jaysh al-Mahdi, Jund al-Khilafah, Ansarullah At-Takfir Val Hidjra, Akromiya, Da'esh, Djabhat An Nusra, Katibat al-Imam al-Buhari, Jannat Oshiqlari, and the Jamaat al-Tawhid wal-Jihad. Authorities also continued the ban on all materials or activities connected to A. A. Tihomirov also known as Said Buryatsky.

On August 8, the Ministry of Justice publicized list of extremist materials banned in the country.

Similar to 2015, numerous human rights activists reported continued arrests and prosecution of persons accused of possessing and distributing Hizb ut-Tahrir literature (see section 1.d.). Most arrests of alleged Hizb ut-Tahrir members occurred in the southern part of the country and involved ethnic Uzbeks. The government charged the majority of those arrested with possession of illegal religious material. In some cases NGOs alleged police planted Hizb ut-Tahrir literature as evidence against those arrested.

c. Freedom of Religion

See the Department of State's *International Religious Freedom Report* at www.state.gov/religiousfreedomreport/.

d. Freedom of Movement, Internally Displaced Persons, Protection of Refugees, and Stateless Persons

The law provides for freedom of internal movement, foreign travel, emigration, and repatriation, and the government generally respected these rights. The law on internal migration provides for freedom of movement. The government generally respected this right, and citizens generally were able to move within the country with relative ease. Certain policies restricted internal migration, resettlement, and travel abroad. The government cooperated with the Office of the UN High Commissioner for Refugees (UNHCR) and other organizations to provide some protection and assistance to refugees, asylum seekers, stateless persons, and other persons of concern.

On August 4, President Atambaev signed an amendment to the law on combating terrorism and extremism that revokes Kyrgyz citizenship of anyone convicted of terrorist and extremist activities.

Foreign Travel: The law on migration prohibits travel abroad by citizens who have or had access to information classified as state secrets until the information is declassified.

Internally Displaced Persons

UNHCR reported there were no internally displaced persons in the country as of September.

Protection of Refugees

As of September UNHCR reported there were 339 refugees in the country. Among mandate and charter refugees, there were 237 from Afghanistan, 60 from Syria, 24 from Uzbekistan, 13 from Ukraine, and five from other countries. There were continued reports of Uzbek refugees seeking refugee status due to fear of abuse by the Uzbek government. In 2015 several of these individuals received status with the state migration authorities, allowing them to remain in the country legally.

Access to Asylum: The law provides for the granting of asylum or refugee status, and the government has established a system for providing protection to refugees. The law on refugees includes nondiscrimination provisions covering persons who were not refugees when they left their country of origin and extends the validity of documents until a final decision on status is determined by a court.

As of late 2015, there were 208 asylum seekers registered with UNHCR in the country. The Ministry of Labor, Migration, and Youth registered 166 asylum seekers, including 84 from Afghanistan, 44 from Uzbekistan, 17 from Ukraine, 12 from Syria, four from Turkmenistan, and smaller numbers from Iran, Pakistan, and Egypt. The other 42 persons were seeking registration from the government at year's end.

Employment: UN-mandated refugees who lacked official status in the country do not have legal permission to work. They were therefore subject to exploitation by employers paying substandard wages, not providing benefits, and not complying with labor regulations. They could not file grievances with authorities. Refugees with official status in the country have legal permission to work.

Access to Basic Services: UN-mandated refugees and asylum seekers who lacked official status were ineligible to receive state-sponsored social benefits. Refugees with official status in the country have access to basic services.

Stateless Persons

UNHCR officials stated the country's stateless persons fell into several categories. As of October 2015, there were an estimated 5,700 Uzbek women who married Kyrgyz citizens but never received Kyrgyz citizenship (many such women allowed their Uzbek passports to expire, and regulations obstructed their efforts to gain Kyrgyz citizenship). Other categories included Roma, individuals with expired Soviet documents, children born to one or both parents who were stateless, and children of migrant workers who renounced their Kyrgyz citizenship in the hope of becoming Russian citizens. The government denied access to social benefits and official work documents to stateless persons, who lacked sufficient legal standing to challenge exploitative labor conditions in court. As of August 1, UNHCR estimated 11,766 stateless persons were living in the country without documents, compared with 10,286 in 2015. The State Registration Service maintained its database of stateless persons based only on those who contacted it.

Of stateless persons registered by UNHCR, 109 were de jure stateless, 1,600 were de facto stateless, 122 were at risk of statelessness, and 623 were persons with undetermined nationality. The latter category is defined by UNHCR as persons who do not have a clearly defined citizenship, comprising mostly Soviet passport holders without birth certificates.

Section 3. Freedom to Participate in the Political Process

The constitution provides citizens the ability to choose their government in free and fair periodic elections held by secret ballot and based on universal and equal suffrage.

Elections and Political Participation

Recent Elections: According to the OSCE Office for Democratic Institutions and Human Rights, the October 2015 parliamentary elections were competitive and provided voters with a wide range of choice. The OSCE concluded that the manner in which the elections were administered, however, reflected the need for improved procedures and increased transparency. During 2015 the government received international support to make all polling stations electronic. Parliament passed a law allowing only those who submitted their biometric data, or fingerprints, to register on the voter rolls. A number of human rights and NGO leaders expressed concern about possible disenfranchisement because of required biometric registration. In September 2015 the constitutional court ruled the biometric registration law constitutional.

Local NGOs deemed December municipal elections "competitive," though reports of technical problems were widespread and media reports alleged isolated incidents of ballot stuffing and other irregularities. The same groups expressed concern about possible misuse of administrative resources to boost voter turnout in a concurrent referendum on amending the constitution.

Political Parties and Political Participation: Members of the 120-seat parliament are selected through a national "party list" system. After voting has occurred, party leaders regularly re-order the lists, often to the disadvantage of women.

Participation of Women and Minorities: There are no legal restrictions on the participation of women in politics. The election code requires the names of male and female candidates be intermixed on party lists and that no more than 70 percent of candidates on a party list can be of the same gender.

By law women must be represented in all branches of government and constitute no less than 30 percent of state bodies and local authorities. The law does not specify the level of the positions at which they must be represented. According to recent statistics from the Inter-Parliamentary Union, 23 percent of the members of parliament were women.

National minorities, who made up 35 percent of the population but held only 10 percent of parliamentary seats, remained underrepresented in both elected and appointed government positions.

Section 4. Corruption and Lack of Transparency in Government

While the law provides criminal penalties for public officials convicted of corruption, the government did not implement the law effectively. Through 2016, there were numerous reports of government officials engaging in corrupt practices, with some instances of officials being held accountable for corruption. The payment of bribes to avoid investigation or prosecution was a major problem at all levels of law enforcement. Law enforcement officers, particularly in the southern part of the country, frequently employed arbitrary arrest, torture, and the threat of criminal prosecution as a means of extorting cash payments from citizens (see section 1.d.).

Corruption: The only government body empowered to investigate corruption was the anticorruption branch of the GKNB. It is not an independent government entity, and its budget remained within the operating budget of the GKNB. The agency's cooperation with civil society was limited, and its investigations led to very few cases going to trial.

As of August the GKNB had investigated 194 criminal corruption cases, of which 13 percent were submitted to court. According to the GKNB, material damage to the government's budget as a result of criminal corruption totaled 1.1 billion som ($16 million). The GKNB reported that 57.8 percent of the damage had been recovered and returned to the national treasury.

On May 30, authorities released Daniyar Narymbaev from detention after his November 2015 conviction of fraud. Narymbaev had been the president's chief of staff prior to his 2015 arrest.

On August 15, the Prosecutor General's Office and the GKNB detained Anvar Mamytov, a former officer of the General Prosecutor's Anti-Corruption Department, on charges of abuse of power and bribery.

Financial Disclosure: The law requires all public officials to publish their income and assets. The State Personnel Service is responsible for making this information public. Officials who do not disclose required information may be dismissed from office, although this punishment was not regularly enforced.

In August the president signed an amendment to the law on the status of judges. The amendment introduced a requirement that judges and candidates for judgeships declare their property, income, and expenditures to deter corruption in the judicial system.

Public Access to Information: The law provides for access to government-held information. All government bodies and local administrative organs are required to establish systems for the release of their operating information to the public. NGOs noted that a wide range of information was available.

Section 5. Governmental Attitude Regarding International and Nongovernmental Investigation of Alleged Violations of Human Rights

Numerous domestic and international human rights organizations operated actively in the country. Nevertheless, governmental actions at times impeded their ability to operate freely.

During a national address in May, the president alleged that two prominent human rights activists belonged to a group working to overthrow the government with the support of foreign secret services. In June the activists filed suit seeking damages and a public apology from the president for "insulting their honor and dignity." In June the court dismissed the suit, and in September the Bishkek City Court rejected the activists' appeal.

The United Nations or Other International Bodies: The government permitted visits by representatives of the United Nations and other organizations in connection with the investigation of abuses or monitoring of human rights problems in the country, including those of the OSCE, ICRC, Norwegian Helsinki Committee, and International Organization for Migration (IOM). The government restricted visits to Azimjon Askarov but otherwise provided international bodies largely unfettered access to civil society activists, detention facilities and detainees, and government officials.

Government Human Rights Bodies: The Office of the Ombudsman acted as an independent advocate for human rights on behalf of private citizens and NGOs and had the authority to recommend cases for court review. During the first half of the year, the office received 37 torture complaints. The atmosphere of impunity surrounding the security forces and their observed ability to act independently against citizens limited the number and type of complaints submitted to the Ombudsman's Office. In 2016, the Ombudsman's Office did not make available statistics regarding the number of complaints it received. The government established the Office of the Ombudsman and National Center to Prevent Torture. The human rights community cooperated with the National Center and effectively conducted routine and unannounced visits to prisons.

Although the Ombudsman's Office exists in part to receive complaints of human rights abuses and pass the complaints to relevant agencies for investigation, both domestic and international observers questioned the office's efficiency. Parliament took steps to restrict the ombudsman's independence, voting in June 2015 to remove ombudsman Baktybek Amanbaev--an action Amanbaev called politically motivated. In December 2015 parliament elected Kubat Otorbaev, a former general director of the state-owned television and broadcasting corporation, as ombudsman.

Section 6. Discrimination, Societal Abuses, and Trafficking in Persons

Women

<u>Rape and Domestic Violence</u>: Rape, including spousal rape, is illegal, but as in previous years, the government failed to enforce the law effectively, and rape cases were underreported. Penalties for conviction of sexual assault range from three to eight years' imprisonment. Prosecutors rarely brought rape cases to court. Statistics for 2016 on the number of cases or convictions were not available. Police generally regarded spousal rape as an administrative, rather than a criminal, offense.

While the law specifically prohibits domestic violence and spousal abuse, violence against women and girls remained a significant problem, yet it was underreported. Penalties for domestic violence convictions range from fines to 15 years' imprisonment, the latter if abuse resulted in death. In 2015 HRW catalogued a range of violent forms of domestic violence and found that the government did not sufficiently investigate and prosecute cases, provide services and support for survivors, pursue protection, or penalize perpetrators. In the small number of reported cases reviewed by courts over recent years, many charges were considered administrative offenses rather than crimes, thus carrying a lesser punishment.

Many crimes against women went unreported due to psychological pressure, economic dependence, cultural traditions, fear of stigma, and apathy among law enforcement officers. There were also reports of spouses retaliating against women who reported abuse.

Several local NGOs provided services to victims of domestic violence, including legal, medical, and psychological assistance, a crisis hotline, shelters, and prevention programs. Organizations assisting battered women also lobbied to streamline the legal process for obtaining protection orders. The government provided offices to the Sezim Shelter for victims of domestic abuse and paid its expenses. According to the shelter, in 2016, its hotline received 1,855 telephone calls, with 91 percent from women.

<u>Other Harmful Traditional Practices</u>: Although prohibited by law, the practice of kidnapping women and girls for forced marriage continued. The Sezim Center reported approximately 50 percent of its clients were in unregistered marriages, which do not have legal force. Observers reported there was a greater frequency of early marriage, polygamy, and bride kidnapping in connection with unregistered religious marriages. This also affected data availability on such marriages.

Some victims of bride kidnapping went to the local police to obtain protective orders, but authorities often poorly enforced such orders. Although in 2012 the government strengthened the penalty for conviction of bride kidnapping to a maximum of 10 years in prison, NGOs continued to report no increase in the reporting or prosecution of the crime.

<u>Sexual Harassment</u>: According to the local NGO Shans, sexual harassment was widespread, especially in private-sector workplaces and among university students, but it rarely was reported or prosecuted. The law prohibits physical sexual assault but not verbal sexual harassment.

<u>Reproductive Rights</u>: By law couples and individuals have the right to decide the number, spacing, and timing of their children; manage their reproductive health; and have access to the information and means to do so, free from discrimination, coercion, and violence. National health regulations require that family planning counseling and services be readily available through a range of health-care professionals, including not only obstetricians and gynecologists but also family doctors, paramedics, and nurse midwives. At the level of primary health care, regulations require that women who request contraceptives receive them regardless of ability to pay.

National health-care protocols require that women be offered postpartum care and counseling on methods and services related to family planning. The government offered special programs to meet the needs of vulnerable target groups, such as adolescents, internally displaced persons, urban migrants, persons in prostitution, and the very poor. In many remote villages, however, reproductive health-care services were unavailable. Where remote services were available, the rugged terrain, inadequate roads, or lack of transport made them nearly inaccessible.

<u>Discrimination</u>: The law provides for the same legal status and rights for women and men, but because of poor enforcement of the law, discrimination against women persisted. The National Council on the Issues of Family, Women, and

Gender Development, which reports to the president, is responsible for women's issues.

As in previous years, data from NGOs working on women's issues indicated women were less healthy, more abused, less able to work outside the home, and less able than men to determine independently the disposition of their earnings. According to the UN Development Fund for Women and domestic NGOs, women did not face discrimination in access to credit or owning businesses.

The annual government-sponsored media campaign to combat violence against women took place from November 25-December 10. According to NGOs, the campaign helped to coordinate the efforts of groups combating violence against women and to publicize the problem nationwide.

Children

Birth Registration: Although the law provides that every child born in the country has the right to receive a birth certificate, local registration, and citizenship, some children were stateless (see section 2.d.). UNHCR reported that children of migrant parents who moved to and acquired citizenship of another country--in many cases, Russia--had to prove both of their parents were Kyrgyz citizens to acquire Kyrgyz citizenship. These children encountered difficulties obtaining citizenship if their parents lacked the necessary documentation.

Education: The law provides for compulsory and free education for the first nine years of schooling or until age 14 or 15. Secondary education is free and universal until age 17. The government did not provide free basic education to all students, and the system of residence registration restricted access to social services, including education for children who were refugees, migrants, or noncitizens. Families who kept children in public schools often paid burdensome and illegal administrative fees.

Child Abuse: Child abuse, including beatings, child labor, and commercial sexual exploitation of boys and girls were problems.

Early and Forced Marriage: Children ages 16 and 17 may legally marry with the consent of local authorities, but the law prohibits civil marriages before the age 16 under all circumstances. Although illegal, the practice of bride kidnapping continued (see section 6, Women). The kidnapping of underage brides remained underreported. The National Statistics Commission estimated that 15 percent of married women between the ages of 25 and 49 married before age 18, and 1 percent under the age of 15. A 2015 HRW report on domestic abuse found inadequate government attention focused on addressing bride kidnapping or other forms of early and forced marriage. In November, the president signed a law criminalizing religious marriages involving minors. Those who violate the law, including parents and religious officiants of such marriages, face prison terms of three to five years.

Sexual Exploitation of Children: The criminal code prohibits the sale of children, child trafficking, child prostitution and child pornography, as well as other sexual crimes against children. The law criminalizes the sale of persons and forced prostitution and provides penalties for conviction of up to 15 years in prison if the victim is a child. The law also makes it a crime to involve someone in prostitution by violence or the threat of violence, blackmail, destroying or damaging property, or fraud. Prosecutors have to prove the element of force, coercion, or fraud in cases of children recruited into prostitution.

The criminal code prohibits the distribution of child pornography and the possession of child pornography with the intent to distribute. The law does not specifically define child pornography, and the criminal code does not fully criminalize computer-related use, access to child pornography online, or simple possession of child pornography.

In 2013 the UN special rapporteur on the sale of children, child prostitution, and child pornography and the UN Children's Fund found that children under age 18 in Bishkek were involved in prostitution. Although precise figures were not known, police stated that typical cases of child prostitution involved young girls from rural areas who relocated to Bishkek for educational opportunities. Once in the capital, they entered the sex trade due to monetary pressures. Additionally, at a Bishkek roundtable on child prostitution, participants discussed the trafficking of young girls for forced labor and commercial sex exploitation. Countries such as the United Arab Emirates, Kazakhstan, China, South Korea, Greece, Turkey, Cyprus, Thailand, Syria, and Germany were mentioned as destination countries for commercial sexual exploitation. There were allegations of law enforcement officials' complicity in human trafficking; police officers allegedly threatened, extorted, and raped child sex-trafficking victims. The government did not investigate the allegations, nor did it prosecute or convict government employees complicit in human trafficking offenses.

The law does not contain an explicit age of consent. Under the criminal code, it is illegal for persons ages 18 and older to have sexual relations with someone under age 16.

<u>Displaced Children</u>: As in previous years, there were numerous reports of child abandonment due to parents' lack of resources, and large numbers of children lived in institutions, foster care, or on the streets. Approximately 80 percent of street children were internal migrants. Street children had difficulty accessing educational and medical services. Police detained street children and sent them home if an address was known or to a rehabilitation center or orphanage. The Rehabilitation Center for Street Children in Bishkek, maintained by the Ministry of Internal Affairs, lacked sufficient food, clothes, and medicine and remained in poor condition.

<u>Institutionalized Children</u>: State orphanages and foster homes lacked resources and often were unable to provide proper care, sometimes resulting in, for example, the transfer of older children to mental health-care facilities even when they did not exhibit mental health problems.

<u>International Child Abductions</u>: The country is a party to the 1980 Hague Convention on the Civil Aspects of International Child Abduction. See the Department of State's *Annual Report on International Parental Child Abduction* at travel.state.gov/content/childabduction/en/legal/compliance.html.

Anti-Semitism

According to NGO Open Position, the Jewish population in the country was approximately 500-700. There were no reports of anti-Semitic comments in the mainstream media.

Trafficking in Persons

See the Department of State's *Trafficking in Persons Report* at www.state.gov/j/tip/rls/tiprpt/.

Persons with Disabilities

The law prohibits discrimination against persons with physical, sensory, intellectual, and mental disabilities, but such persons faced discrimination in employment, education, air travel and other transportation, access to health care, the judicial system, and the provision of other state services. The law mandates access to buildings for persons with disabilities, requires access to public transportation and parking, and authorizes subsidies to make mass media available to persons with hearing or vision disabilities, and free plots of land for the construction of a home. The government generally did not ensure proper implementation of the law. In addition, persons with disabilities often had difficulty finding employment because of negative societal attitudes and high unemployment among the general population.

A lack of government resources made it difficult for persons with disabilities to receive adequate education. Although children with disabilities have the right to an education, the Association of Parents of Children with Disabilities stated schools often denied them entry. The government funded programs to provide school supplies and textbooks to children with mental or physical disabilities.

As in previous years, conditions at psychiatric hospitals were substandard, stemming largely from inadequate funding. The government did not adequately provide for basic needs, such as food, water, clothing, heating, and health care, and facilities were often overcrowded.

Authorities usually placed children with mental disabilities in psychiatric hospitals rather than integrating them with other children. Other residents were also committed involuntarily, including children without mental disabilities who were too old to remain in orphanages. The Youth Human Rights Group monitored the protection of children's rights in institutions for children with mental and physical disabilities. The group previously noted gross violations by staff at several institutions, including depriving young residents of sufficient nourishment and physically abusing them.

The Office of the Prosecutor General is responsible for protecting the rights of psychiatric patients and persons with disabilities. According to local NGO lawyers, members of the Prosecutor General's Office had no training and little knowledge of the protection of these rights and were ineffective in assisting citizens with disabilities. Most judges lacked the experience and training to make determinations as to whether it was appropriate to mandate committing persons to psychiatric hospitals, and authorities institutionalized individuals against their will.

Several activists noted authorities had not implemented a 2008 law requiring employers to provide special hiring quotas (approximately 5 percent of work positions) for persons with disabilities.

National/Racial/Ethnic Minorities

Tensions between ethnic Uzbeks, who comprised nearly half the population in the southern Osh oblast, and ethnic Kyrgyz in the oblast, as well as elsewhere in the southern part of the country, remained problematic. Discrimination against ethnic Uzbeks in business and government, as well as harassment and reported arbitrary arrests of ethnic Uzbeks, illustrated these tensions. Ethnic Uzbeks reported large public works and road construction projects undertaken without public consultation interfered with neighborhoods and destroyed homes.

The Concept for the Development of National Unity and Inter-Ethnic Relations in the Kyrgyz Republic continued to be the main document promoting reconciliation between ethnic Kyrgyz and Uzbek communities in the southern part of the country. The goal is to spread the use of Kyrgyz as a unifying state language while also promoting multilingualism and instilling respect for the rights of minority groups. At year's end the concept had not been fully implemented.

Acts of Violence, Discrimination, and Other Abuses Based on Sexual Orientation and Gender Identity

LGBTI persons whose sexual orientation or gender identity was publicly known risked physical and verbal abuse, possible loss of jobs, and unwanted attention from police and other authorities. Inmates and officials often openly victimized incarcerated gay men. Some members of the LGBTI community said their families ostracized them when they learned of their sexual orientation or gender identity. Forced marriages of lesbians and bisexual women to men also occurred. The Labrys Public Foundation noted the continued practice of "corrective rape" of lesbians to "cure" their homosexuality.

Labrys, Kyrgyz Indigo, and Grace--three established LGBTI support NGOs-- reported numerous acts of violence against members of the LGBTI community. In October a LGBTI assistance office in Osh was firebombed by several men who threw Molotov cocktails through the window of the office. No one was injured in the attack, but the interior of the office was damaged. NGO representatives said police who arrived on scene seemed to focus on the activities of the office instead of finding the perpetrators.

Members of the LGBTI community reported an increase in attempts to forcibly "out" gays and lesbians on social media. In the spring a transgender woman was surrounded by three men who verbally and physically harassed and threatened her if she did not pay them money while one in the group recorded her. With the help of an NGO, she pressed charges against the three men, but she dropped the case after the men threatened her. After the case was settled out of court, the recording was uploaded on social media.

In 2014 HRW released a report based on interviews with 40 LGBTI persons chronicling instances of extortion, beatings, and sexual assault. The report described in detail how police patrolling parks and bars frequented by gay men would threaten them with violence and arrest or threaten to reveal their homosexuality to their families if they did not pay bribes. These practices, according to representatives of the LGBTI community, continued in 2016. NGO leaders in the southern part of the country reported an even greater threat.

HIV and AIDS Social Stigma

While the law protects against discrimination and stigmatization of persons with HIV/AIDS, according to a 2012 national demographic and health survey, a majority of respondents reported discriminatory attitudes towards those living with HIV.

Section 7. Worker Rights

a. Freedom of Association and the Right to Collective Bargaining

The law provides workers the right to form and join trade unions. The law allows unions to conduct their activities without interference and provides them the right to organize and bargain collectively. Workers may strike, but the requirement to receive formal approval made striking difficult and complicated. The law on government service prohibits government employees from striking, but the prohibition does not apply to teachers or medical professionals. The law does not prohibit retaliation against striking workers.

Many unions reportedly operated as quasi-official institutions that took state interests into consideration rather than representing workers' interests exclusively. The Federation of Trade Unions (FTU) remained the only umbrella trade union in the country. Unions were not required to belong to the FTU, and there were several smaller unaffiliated unions.

The government effectively enforced these rights. Workers exercised their right to join and form unions, and unions exercised the right to organize and bargain collectively. Union leaders, however, generally cooperated with the government, and international observers judged that unions represented the interests of their members poorly. In past years some unions alleged unfair dismissals of union leaders and the formation of single-company unions.

b. Prohibition of Forced or Compulsory Labor

The law prohibits all forms of forced or compulsory labor. The law specifically prohibits the use of force, fraud, or coercion for the purpose of sex or labor exploitation and prescribes penalties for conviction of five to 20 years' imprisonment for violations. Forced labor is also prohibited by the labor code and the code on children. The government did not fully implement legal prohibitions, and victim identification remained a concern.

The Ministry of Labor provided a toll-free telephone line to the IOM to provide information to potential migrants and to help victims of labor trafficking. According to the IOM, approximately 2,500 persons used the hotline through September.

There were cases of forced labor, including of children (see section 7.c.).

Also see the Department of State's *Trafficking in Persons Report* at www.state.gov/j/tip/rls/tiprpt/.

c. Prohibition of Child Labor and Minimum Age for Employment

The law sets the minimum legal age for basic employment at 16, except for work performed without a signed employment contract or work considered to be "light," such as selling newspapers, in which children as young as age 14 may work with the permission of a parent or guardian. The law prohibits employment of persons under age 18 at night, underground, or in difficult or dangerous conditions, including in the metal, oil, and gas industries; mining and prospecting; the food industry; entertainment; and machine building. Children ages 14 or 15 may work up to five hours a day; children ages 16 to 18 may work up to seven hours a day. These laws also apply to children with disabilities. Violation of the law incurs penalties ranging from fines to imprisonment of up to 10 years, depending on the nature and severity of the offense. Enforcement and prosecution of violations continued to pose challenges to deterrence.

Despite some advancement in efforts to eliminate the worst forms of child labor, child labor remained a problem. According to recent reports, children continued to be engaged in agricultural work in cotton cultivation, as well as selling and transporting goods at bazaars.

The Prosecutor General's Office and the State Labor Inspectorate are responsible for enforcing employers' compliance with the labor code. Inspectors conducted infrequent and ineffective child labor inspections. Since many children worked for their families or were self-employed, it was difficult for the government to determine whether work complied with the labor code.

See also the Department of Labor's *Findings on the Worst Forms of Child Labor* at www.dol.gov/ilab/reports/child-labor/findings/.

d. Discrimination with Respect to Employment and Occupation

The law prohibits discrimination with respect to employment and occupation on the basis of sex, race, ethnicity, language, origin, property, official status, age, place of residence, religion, and political convictions, membership in public organizations, or other circumstances irrelevant to professional capacities. The government did not effectively enforce applicable law, and the nature of penalties for conviction of violations was insufficient to deter violations. Uzbeks in the south also complained it was hard to start a small business due to discriminatory practices in licensing and registering a business with the local authorities.

Average wages for women were substantially less than for men. Women made up the majority of pensioners, a group particularly vulnerable to deteriorating economic conditions. In rural areas traditional attitudes toward women limited them to the roles of wife and mother and curtailed educational opportunities. Members of the LGBTI community reported discrimination in the work place when they were open about their sexual orientation. Persons with disabilities were subjected to discrimination in hiring and access to the workplace.

e. Acceptable Conditions of Work

The official national minimum monthly wage was 1,060 som ($15). Employers generally paid somewhat higher wages. The law on minimum wage states it should rise gradually to meet the cost of living. The National Statistics Committee reported the average monthly salary was 13,190 som ($191).

The standard workweek is 40 hours, usually within a five-day week. For state-owned industries, there is a mandated 24-hour rest period in a seven-day workweek. According to the labor code, overtime work cannot exceed four hours per day or 20 hours per week, and workers must receive compensatory leave or premium pay of between 150 and 200 percent of the hourly wage. These provisions were mainly enforced at large companies and organizations with strong trade unions. Employees of small and informal firms fall under the law but generally had no union representation.

The National Statistics Committee defined informal economic activity as household units that produce goods and services primarily to provide jobs and income to their members. The government estimated only 24 percent of the population worked in the formal sector of the economy while the rest worked in the informal economy.

Safety and health conditions in factories were poor. The law establishes occupational health and safety standards, but the government generally did not enforce them. Penalties for violation of the law include community service to fines ranging from 500 to 5,000 som ($7.20 to $72) and up to 10 years' imprisonment. The law does not provide workers the right to remove themselves from a hazardous workplace without jeopardizing their employment. The State Labor Inspectorate is responsible for protecting workers and carrying out inspections for all types of labor problems. According to the State Inspectorate, there were 27 labor inspectors, but their activities were limited, and business compliance was uneven. The law does not provide for occupational health and safety standards for workers in the informal economy.

Government licensing rules placed strict requirements on companies recruiting citizens to work abroad, and the Ministry of Labor, Migration, and Youth licensed such companies. The government regularly published a list of licensed and vetted firms. Recruiters were required to monitor employer compliance with employment terms and the working conditions of labor migrants while under contract abroad. Recruiters were also required to provide workers with their employment contract prior to their departure.

The government took steps to streamline labor migration by adopting a program on the regulation of migration processes and collaborating with the governments of Russia, the Republic of Korea, and Kazakhstan to improve the protection of the rights of Kyrgyz labor migrants working abroad.